Grow Curious

This book belongs to:

----

ex libris --- ex hortus

Grow Curious

A Journal to Cultivate Wonder in Your Garden and Beyond

Gayla Trail

With illustrations by Davin Risk

CHRONICLE BOOKS

SAN FRANCISCO

Manufactured in China.

ISBN 978-1-7972-0986-9

10 9 8 7 6 5 4 3 2 1

Chronicle books and gifts are available at special
quantity discounts to corporations, professional
associations, literacy programs, and other
organizations. For details and discount information,
please contact our premiums department at
corporatesales@chroniclebooks.com or
at 1-800-759-0190.

Chronicle Books LLC
680 Second Street
San Francisco, California 94107
www.chroniclebooks.com

To my favorite mammals—Davin and Molly—who
share and delight in the life of the garden with me.

Contents

Sow seed.
Grow food.
Touch plants.
Put my feet
on the earth.

Introduction

A few days after I began working on this book, North America went into lockdown to prevent the spread of the coronavirus, COVID-19. In one dramatic sweep, the world shifted for all of us. It was mid-March and the garden was just beginning to come to life after what had been, for me, a long and difficult winter. I understood immediately that the garden would be the solid ground I'd need to get through whatever was to come, and, more than ever, I'd be throwing myself into it as a place of sanctuary.

Each spring, I tend to plant far too much for my narrow, urban yard. I'm a more-is-more person as it is—an overstuffed garden is my default. (By summer, the garden is always a dense and wild space with very little room to move. I mean that without one iota of hyperbole.) Still, when the pandemic started, I doubled my seed-starting efforts anyway, pulling countless packets of seed, old and new, out of my extensive seed bank/hoard. I was going to throw everything I had at this virus, planting, growing, and gardening my way through it with enough excess seedlings to supply friends, family, and beyond.

Sow seed. Grow food. Touch plants. Put my feet on the earth. These words emerged like a mantra—a recipe for staying sane and focusing on the present at a time when the future was unpredictable and a bit scary. But really, when isn't life unpredictable and a bit scary? Being human, navigating our way through the seasons of our lives can be hard, pandemic or not.

If you're reading this, perhaps you feel the same. Perhaps you recognize that we need plants—for food, medicine, and oxygen, yes, but it's more than that. Gardening is an act of reciprocal nurturing: By tending the soil and the plants, we are tending to ourselves in return.

Gardening is a relationship, an affectionate dialogue with the earth. Or, at least it can be.

For me, the garden is a place of grounding and strength. When life gets harried, it is where I go in order to return to myself. Working with the seasons has taught me how to be more in tune with them, to live more closely with nature, and to find my place within it. It has given me a place to enact my deep need to nurture safely and comfortably, and, in unearthing my tenderness, the garden has nurtured me back. I think I am the garden's mother, but in truth, she is mine.

We belong to nature and are not separate from it, but for many, a relationship with this core part of ourselves has been neglected. Cultivating and communing with plants can be a way to rekindle that relationship, tend to it, and learn it again, like a language spoken long ago, but not forgotten.

Gardening is for all of us.

Using This Book

This journal is an invitation to play. To get curious about your garden and engage with your creativity. To spend time learning about nature and, in turn, yourself.

This book is not a demand. We have enough of that in our lives as it is. There is one activity, however, that I prefer you start with. I have handily titled it "Begin Here." Please do. Once you have completed it, feel free to jump around and choose your own adventure.

There are activities to engage you on multiple levels—to create and gather, to inspire exploration and experimentation, and to challenge the way you think about and see your garden. Flip through until you come upon a project that calls you to action. When you find one that speaks to you or moves you in some way, do it repeatedly. When you're done with the activities you like most, come back to those that didn't appeal to you initially, because your perspective or circumstances may have changed over time.

Several creative activities in this book ask you to sketch, draw, or take photos of what you see. These projects are open to everyone and are not just meant for "creative types." Even if drawing or photography is not your thing, I hope you will give them (and yourself) a chance. Use crayons or markers if that's what you prefer. Spend 20 seconds on a drawing or hours. How far you take it is up to you. The goal here is more about playing and looking closely than it is about making a "good" piece of art.

The gardening year flows in tandem with the cycles and rhythms of life as we move from birth (spring) through to stasis (winter). I have followed that pattern, with activities assigned to each season. However, many of them are universal and will work year-round. If you find one in winter that you would really like to do in the spring, go for it. Or, simply wander through your garden and look; sit and listen. There is more to learn in the garden than how to grow a tomato. Much, much more.

Regardless of size, style, or location, the garden is a place of transformation and wonder. Something exciting is always happening there. All you have to do is look for it.

Your Time

In the world of adults, there are kids to feed, jobs to go to, dogs to walk, bills to pay, life to live. Some days there isn't enough time to take care of the garden let alone to cultivate joy, wonder, and discovery there. Make as much time as you can given your circumstances. One minute. Ten minutes. An hour.

I've included quick and easy projects as well as long-term assignments so that you can choose what works for your schedule. Some projects continue beyond their original scope with ideas to "Go Further," depending on your time, interest, and what you feel you can handle. Many of the observational-type activities can be done while you are undertaking garden chores, harvesting the carrots, or watering the tomatoes. Make mental notes if you don't have the tools on hand to make physical ones. Take 5 extra seconds while you're working to explore the terrain of a single leaf, smell the air, taste a flower. Slow down. Take it all in.

How much time do you need to devote to these activities? As much or as little time as you like. Projects can be done and completed on your own schedule, without pressure. Put the journal down and pick it back up again as many times as you need. Come back to it next week, next season, next year. There is no shame in taking breaks, going slow, or skipping activities that push you in directions you can't or don't want to go. Feel free to adjust projects to your abilities or skip them altogether. After all, this is a book about embracing who you are, where you are now. Start there.

What You Need

Most of the activities in this journal call for simple materials: this journal and a favorite writing implement. Keep both on hand—in your bag, in the garden, in a shed, by the front or back door, or somewhere else within easy reach.

Other Tools

Besides the writing and drawing tools, most of the items on this list are entirely optional:

- Writing, drawing, and painting tools (colored markers, pens, pencils, pastels, crayons, watercolor paint, etc.)
- Camera (cell phone, digital, film, disposable, etc.)
- Magnifying glass (a cheap kid's one or the magnification feature on a smartphone will do)
- Small envelopes
- Tape (masking, washi, etc.)

Begin Here

We gardeners rarely give ourselves the time and space to experience our gardens without working toward a goal: prune the raspberries, sow the carrots, deadhead the roses. We are always doing. Sometimes doing can get in the way of seeing and being. The garden becomes a job with a list of tasks affixed to it rather than a place to connect with nature.

Carve out 5 to 10 minutes (or more if you can) to observe your garden. Walk around, stand still, or pull up a stool and sit quietly. Refrain from all chores or thoughts of them if you can. Shutting off the impulse to putter might be extremely difficult for you. I know it is for me.

Note: If your garden is a small balcony, fire escape, or somewhere else without "walking around" space, pull up a stool, sit on the ground, or stand in a spot that gives you visual access to the entire garden. Use your eyes rather than your limbs to do the walking.

○ Under the appropriate seasonal header, write down any observations that come to mind. A few small details are enough. For example: a bird chirping, a newly emerged flower, dewdrops on a leaf.

○ Write about how it felt (in the mind and body) to let go and do nothing during that block of time. Was it difficult or easy? Were there physical sensations in the letting go?

Go Further

Repeat this exercise each season.

Season: _____

_____

_____

_____

_____

_____

_____

_____

_____

_____

_____

_____

_____

_____

_____

_____

_____

_____

_____

_____

_____

_____

_____

_____

_____

_____

Season:

Season: _____

_____
_____
_____
_____
_____
_____
_____
_____
_____
_____
_____
_____
_____
_____
_____
_____
_____
_____
_____
_____
_____
_____
_____
_____
_____
_____
_____

Season: _____

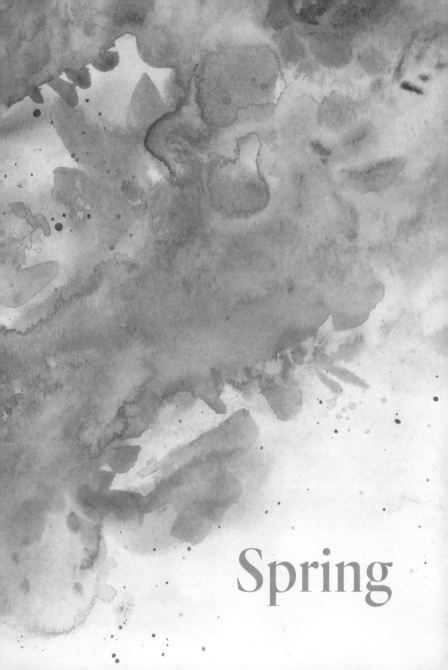

Spring

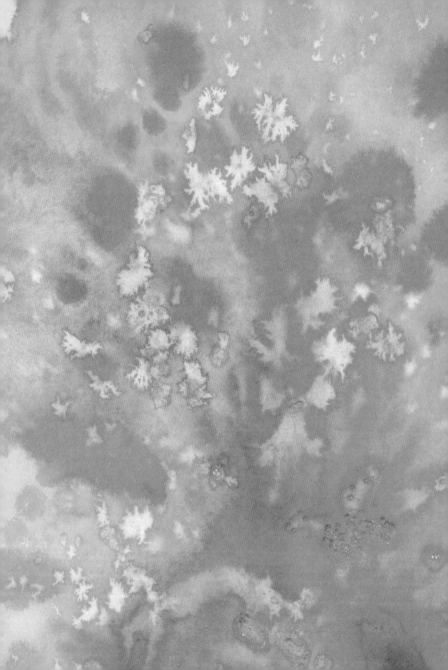

This Is It

This is when it begins. It's there now, but you have to look for it. Be a detective. Turn your attention to the soil. Can you see it? Today you may have to crouch down and push some debris away to get the smallest glimpse, but within just a few weeks it will all be happening with such ferocity and speed that you will beg for it to slow down so you can catch your breath.

There is something universal about springtime that invites us all into a mindset of hope, transformation, and optimism. Like the garden, our bodies are pulled to move and expand, lit up with the energy of renewal. This is when I dive into the garden like a madwoman who has been locked indoors for 4 months, chewing off my own arm, because, except for that last part, I have been. I must get outside. I must grow all the things! And I do. Trays and trays of things, which I will come to regret in the summer when I have to find a home for them all. But there are no regrets in spring. Only little green friends, the smell of moist earth, and the promise of beauty and bounty to come.

When spring arrives, it makes an entrance. One minute the world is barren and lifeless. The moment conditions are right, seedlings carpet the soil's surface. Plants don't wait for you to get your bearings or catch up. They seize that right moment—their moment—and then they are off.

Spring's flowers are some of the best of the year, but they are fleeting. They catch the first wave of warmth and manage to live out an entire life cycle in the blink of an eye. There's a lesson in this that we can learn from plants: Don't hesitate. Don't hold back. Grab your moment. Go all out and thrive.

One Word

On a piece of loose paper, write down a single word that describes your garden. Don't get too hung up on it. Just write the first word that pops into your head. Write the date on the front of a small envelope and seal the piece of paper with your word inside. Tape it to the facing page.

Go Further

Repeat this activity next year around the same time. Open last year's envelope. How does this year's word compare with last year's?

Emerging

Sketch, paint, or photograph the first plant that pops up in the spring.

New Introductions

Make a list of every plant (including transplants, cuttings, and seeds) that you plan to introduce into your garden this year.

○ Why these plants? Do they serve an intentional goal? (For example, are they for native bees, a certain color, drought tolerant, or edibles?)

○ At the end of the spring season, come back to this page and answer the following: Which will you grow again?

Go Further

One year later, check off the plants that remain or that produced seeds for next year.

Fear and Insecurity

If I had a dollar for every aspiring gardener who confided in me that they can't or really shouldn't be a gardener . . .

"But I kill plants," they whisper. "I only have a tiny balcony. When would I find the time? Don't I need to buy a lot of tools and stuff? I don't know where to begin. I'm scared of messing it up."

The truth is, except for the few who are fortunate to learn the ins and outs under the wing of an experienced gardener, we all begin in the same place—feeling silly and clueless, but hungry with the desire to nurture some little green thing.

I can tell you now, with decades of experience behind me, gardening is not a calling reserved strictly for the landowner or homeowner, for people who have money, or for those with magical green thumbs. Gardening is for everyone!

○ Write your fears on this page. Now, tear out the page and bury it in a hole in your garden. If you don't have a garden in the ground, bury it in the bottom of a flowerpot. Plant something on top. Let it rot!

As I tend
the garden,
the garden
tends to me.

Reunited

My first plant was a little parsley grown from seed in a Styrofoam cup. I was 5 years old, and I still remember the excitement I felt every time I went to check on it. As an adult, I always keep some parsley in the garden. It's such a simple, overlooked herb, but it never fails to bring me back to my childhood self.

- Do you have memories (from your childhood or later in life) of a flower or plant that intrigued you or maybe even sowed the seed of your gardening life? Your assignment is to grow it now, either from a transplant or seed.
- Write about the experience of regrowing an old plant friend. Does it conjure specific memories or emotions?

Go Further

Did you have a connection to nature in childhood? Was there a time in your life when it was lost? Why do you think that happened?

Make Plant Ink

Extracting color from the leaves, roots, flowers, fruits, and seeds of plants to make dyes, inks, and paints is a different way to experience the seasons of your garden and the varied color palette therein. What colors will the distinct parts of each plant make and when is the best season to harvest them? The answers to these questions will depend on the unique growing conditions in your space and the soil there.

Through the years, I've been using the leaves, flowers, and fruits of common plants, such as stinging nettle, goldenrod, coreopsis, and elderberry, from my small urban garden to dye fabric and thread for textile projects. Plant inks that you can paint, draw, and write with aren't much different from dyes; they're just made in smaller, more concentrated batches. These microbatches have proven to be particularly exciting because they require little effort or plant material to capture extraordinary color, while making dyes can require armfuls of fresh plant material that needs to be cooked for longer periods of time. Once you start, you realize that just about every plant in the garden is a possible source material. Even better, the end product is only as toxic as the plants you use, making it possible to produce safe inks for kids to use too.

Some plants produce ink with a color similar to their original state. For example, fresh stinging nettle and mint leaves make greens reminiscent of their leaves. Others, however, can develop in some wild ways. I was surprised to find that ink made by crushing red and orange tulips in white vinegar initially appeared red on paper, but it dried as bright green. The dull yellow ink from daffodil flowers is decent enough, but I was shocked to find that the first swatch I painted transformed overnight into the most vibrant, almost neon yellow. Plants are magic!

How to Make Ink

There are a lot of ways to make ink and no one "right" method. How simple or complicated you make it is your choice.

Method One

Toss some plant material into a pot (see Note on page 42), add just enough water to cover the top of the plant bits, and cook over low heat on the stove. There are no exact measurements or cooking times. It all depends on the plant material and the amount available. Just pay attention, making test swatches along the way, and stop when the color is pleasing. Strain out the plant material through a coffee filter; discard the plant material, reserving the liquid. Cook the liquid down further if the batch is too watery, or stop here and bottle it in sterilized jars. You can thicken ink that's too thin with powdered or liquid gum arabic (a natural sap from the acacia tree). This is especially useful for writing inks, but since I tend to paint with them, I prefer mine without.

To prevent your ink from going moldy, add to the final jar your choice of preservative: white vinegar (about 1 tsp per cup); wintergreen essential oil (a drop per cup); high-proof alcohol (such as Everclear or vodka) or rubbing alcohol (about 1 tsp per cup); a pinch of thyme; or a couple of whole cloves. (Note that vinegar will likely modify the color—but this can be a fun experiment!) Most inks will last a few weeks or even months if stored in the fridge.

Method Two

Instead of cooking on the stove, crush fresh leaves or petals with a mortar and pestle (or the handle of a wooden spoon in a jar). Strain out the solids and add in a pinch of salt and a couple of splashes of pure white vinegar. Be aware that the high acid content will modify the color of some plants. That said, it's a lot easier than the cooking method and can produce some fantastically bright colors, especially from flowers such as periwinkle, daffodil, violet, and tulip.

Note: Caution. Unless you are using only edible plant parts, set aside any utensils, pots, or containers that you use for ink-making purposes; some common plants, such as daffodil flowers, are quite poisonous.

Plants to Try

Red
pokeberry, sumac berry, rose hip, beetroot, hibiscus flower

Purple
elderberry, wild grape, purple cabbage, mulberry, quince flower

Yellow
goldenrod flower, golden beetroot, rhubarb root, onion skin

Green
stinging nettle, mint, woad, spinach, grass

Blue
muscari flower (add vinegar), huckleberry, periwinkle flower (add vinegar)

Brown
black walnut, dandelion root, various tree barks

Use the boxes below to swatch and label the plant inks you make.

Gardening Body

Gardening is a physical act, but most of us do not pay attention to the ways we experience it in our bodies. Bring this book into the garden with you, and as you go about various tasks, pay attention to where you feel it most in your body. Working the actions in slow motion can help. Now, stop and take a few long, deep breaths.

On the body outline on the facing page, circle the areas where you feel the strongest sensations, making note of each corresponding activity, such as digging a hole or deadheading. Which muscles and muscle groups are most often engaged? In which areas do you brace or tighten? Where do you feel release and relief?

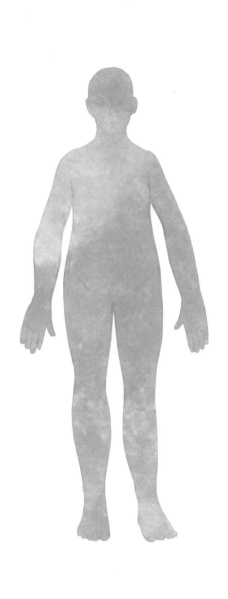

Sketch of the Month

Choose a plant and draw a quick sketch of it in one of the boxes provided every month until it dies, goes into dormancy, or you've filled all the boxes.

○ What did you learn about the plant from observing it so closely?

Take a Chance

Every spring I draw up a very rough plan for the growing season based on what we need and want to eat. I also leave space for impulse: some new and compelling plant or variety that I hadn't planned for and don't really need, but simply must grow.

Obviously we can't always have everything we want, but at times these moments of happenstance have changed my gardening experience in profound ways that I could not have predicted. For example, when I started my current garden, I brought along a handful of *Aquilegia* (columbines) from my old community garden. That spring, I acquired several more from friends and plant sales. I had never intended to introduce so many into the garden—it just happened. With time, the plants began to cross-pollinate, producing all kinds of fascinating and completely new combinations. A decade in, I am enraptured by these simple plants and eagerly await their bloom in late spring. They have become an unexpected source of pleasure and intense botanical learning. Had I stuck to hard and fast plans, I would not have had this experience.

This spring, leave some wiggle room for chance in your planting decisions. Adopt an unusual, just-for-fun plant or two that you would not have considered otherwise.

○ Write about what compelled you to choose this plant. Were you drawn to its look, scent, or history, or to a story you heard about it?

_____

_____

_____

_____

_____

_____

_____

_____

_____

_____

At the end of the season, come back and answer the following:

○ List 2 things you learned through the process of growing it.

_____

_____

_____

_____

_____

○ Will you grow this plant again? Why or why not?

_____

_____

_____

_____

_____

Seedling ID

Mystery plants show up in my garden beds each year. Some are volunteers from nearby gardens that hitch a ride via birds, mammals, and soil that comes in from new plants. Others are returning self-seeders. Being able to identify a range of plants in the seedling stage prevents me from weeding out what I want to keep and allows me to remove those I don't before they take hold.

In the spaces provided, draw 3 seedlings directly after germination, when they only have their "seed leaves" (the embryonic leaves that appear before "true leaves" develop). The seedlings can be those you've sown, purchased, or found growing in the garden or a pot.

Sketch the seedlings again in a week or two once their first true leaves develop. If the seedling is a mystery, search online or use a plant ID app (see Resources on page 222) to identify it. You may find it easier to recognize and categorize the plant once true leaves have come in.

Seedling One

Seedling Two

Seedling Three

Invite Wildness

Wildness is everywhere, even in cities. We can find it, connect to it, and become its steward exactly where we are, no matter where we live. It is around us and within us. All it takes is an adjustment in perspective.

In my current garden, the process of wilding came about as a personal response to a touch of perfectionism that I couldn't quite shake from my gardening practice. We carry a lot of cultural baggage into the garden with us—our own expectations as well as those of our community and society as a whole. Despite years as a confident gardener, I felt conflicted by the experimental, playful, and spontaneous style that I had developed and ashamed that I could not—would not—conform to the orderly and unblemished (yet with an acceptable hint of lived-in character) garden that has become sacrosanct in our Pinterest culture. There were moments in the beginning of my wilding process when I felt anxious and uneasy, as if letting go, however purposeful and intentional, would lead to chaos.

As the garden evolved, however, I was able to see that we (both the garden and I) were not becoming uncultivated or unhinged. Instead, we were unfolding and transforming into something new and more honest: flawed, aware, complex, and resilient. Beneficial insects visited in numbers I have never experienced before. They brought with them an aliveness that I did not know had been missing. With time, the fear slipped away and I felt at ease in the rhythmic, spontaneous dance of diversity in the garden. There was new confidence and pride as I experienced the richness and complexity of having kinship with a place that I had a hand in shaping. Plants thrived, creatures thrived, I thrived.

"Wild" and "cultivated" are social constructs that we place in opposition to each other, when in reality there is a knotty labyrinth between them. We subjugate our cities and our gardens with chemicals and artifice because we are unable to see that wild and cultivated can be entwined, can be all at once tended, lyrical, surprising, domesticated, irrational, functional, and free.

Ways to Invite Wildness into the Garden

Introduce nectar and pollen-rich flowers that will attract bees, butterflies, wasps, and other beneficial insects. Examples include borage, allium, *Agastache*, clover, dandelion, salvia, dill, fennel, *Liatris*, and goldenrod.

Be less tidy. Rather than rushing to clean up, allow some plants to grow bigger and bushier. Create small piles of old branches and leave them to decompose and become a haven for lichen, moss, fungi, and insects (which will become a food source for insectivorous birds). On a balcony or terrace, a container of soil and dead wood will have the same effect.

Set aside a section of garden as an undisturbed meadow or an area of long grass. Allow plants to set seed and die back with the seasons and watch what happens. You can even do this on a small scale in a container or old kiddie pool (punch holes in the bottom for drainage).

Give up using pesticides, herbicides, and chemical fertilizers. These products do long-term damage for short-term results, and even the organic ones are sometimes toxic to beneficial soil organisms, insects, and other critters. Instead, work toward building a holistic ecosystem that includes healthy soil and a diverse range of plant and insect species.

Add a source of water. Ponds are great if you have the space, but even a shallow dish of fresh water on a hot day can be a source of hydration for insects, amphibians, reptiles, and mammals. Refresh the water daily to avoid breeding mosquitos.

Research plants that are native to your region and introduce species suitable to your growing conditions.

Stop digging and double digging the soil. Add compost and other soil amendments to the soil surface and mix them in lightly using your fingers or a fork.

Ensure that there are flowers in bloom throughout the growing season, especially at the beginning and end when pollen sources are scarce.

Don't cut dried plant stalks. Insects and birds alight upon them. Spiders use them as web supports. Other critters live inside them and still others use them as materials for building their habitats.

○ How can you bring more wildness to an outdoor space this year? Jot down a few notes here.

Putting Out Roots

A few years ago, a friend and I grew the same plant. We regularly checked in with each other throughout the growing season to compare their progress. In the fall, when my friend dug up the plant's root system, he noticed that the roots were growing very deliberately toward a nearby patch of red clover, a nitrogen-fixing plant that releases nitrogen into the soil. We hypothesized that perhaps the plant was reaching toward the clover in search of nourishment and support.

○ In your garden, have you ever noticed a plant growing toward or in some way relying on another?

_____

_____

_____

_____

○ If you had roots, what or whom would you grow toward for nourishment and support?

_____

_____

_____

_____

_____

_____

_____

_____

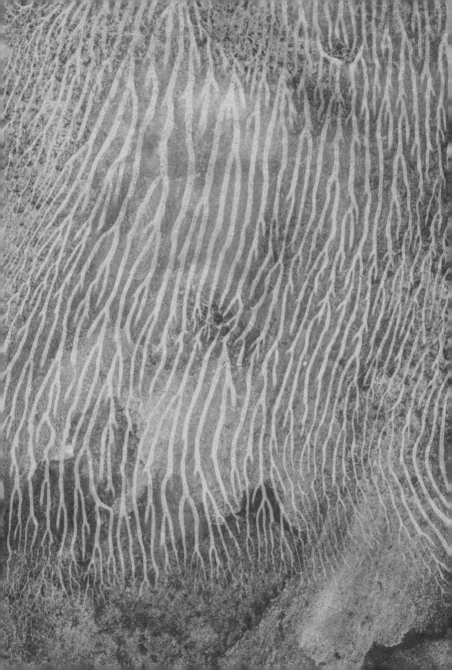

Scavenger Hunt

Search your garden for one example from each of the following categories and write short descriptions of what you find. Optionally, draw, doodle, or even trace them in the space provided.

- New leaf or flower bud
- Fully open flower
- Seed or seedpod
- Dry, old leaf
- Insect

Go Further

Repeat this exercise every month for a full year. Don't feel obligated to draw them all. You may be surprised by what you can find during the harshest seasons.

The Scent of Rain

Microbiologists attribute petrichor (the delicious, fresh odor of rain as it hits dry soil) to bacteria that produce an organic compound called geosmin. The theory is that the scent attracts tiny arthropods called springtails that live in leaf litter and eat organic waste. When the springtails feed on this bacterium, they help to complete its life cycle, spreading the organism far and wide.

○ Go outside and explore the garden on a rainy day. Breathe in deeply. Smell the soil. Smell your plants. Soak it all in.

○ Visit the garden again once the sun has come out or on a warm morning after a particularly heavy rainstorm. Has the look of the plants changed? Have fallen plants perked up? Has their smell changed?

Your Palette

Make swatches in the provided space of some of the colors that are in your garden right now. Use markers, crayons, or paints. List words beside each that describe the colors. If the palette is too extensive to record, focus on the dominant colors or stick to one section of the garden.

Go Further

Return to this activity monthly to create a color palette for the whole year.

Garden Doodle

Now that you've determined your color palette, sketch out a loose likeness of your garden. Rather than drawing for form or accuracy, quickly scribble where each color occurs. Scrawl larger or smaller areas to approximate the amount of each color as it occurs in the scene. For example, a patch of strawberry plants in bloom might be represented by lots of green with white dots.

It may help to squint your eyes first so that your vision is fuzzy and objects blur (or, if you're myopic like me, just remove your glasses!). Be messy and loose. The goal here is not to draw the actual plants, but to create an image that functions as more of a color chart than a drawing.

Smell Everything

We're all drawn to smell the flowers, but how often do you smell the leaves of plants that aren't known herbs? Pepper plants, started from seed in the spring, are a mainstay in my summer garden. For many years, it didn't occur to me that the foliage could have a smell. Wow, was I surprised! It wasn't a peppermint or basil leaf smell, but it had a unique and rather pleasant scent. From that moment on, I resolved to get a whiff of every plant I grow. It's been a surprising education and a way to know plants more intimately.

This year, resolve to "scratch and sniff" the foliage of every plant in your indoor and outdoor garden. You may be surprised by what you discover.

○ List any unusual discoveries here and describe their scent.

Last Days of Spring

Watch for these signs and check them off:

☐ Warmer days and nights

☐ Longer days

☐ More active birds and other creatures

☐ Appearance of new birds and other creatures in the garden

☐ Emergence of new and warm-season plants

☐ Full leaves on deciduous trees

☐ Less rain (this is less predictable with global warming)

☐ Cool weather salad greens (especially spinach and lettuce) that bolt (meaning the plants grow taller and/or produce flowers)

○ Write down any other signs that you have noticed. Depending on your climate, you may discover that cooler season crops, such as lettuce and other leafy greens, are bolting as they prepare to produce seed, and that self-seeding plants that like warmer soil, such as borage and shiso, are beginning to pop up where they grew in previous years.

Additional Notes from Spring

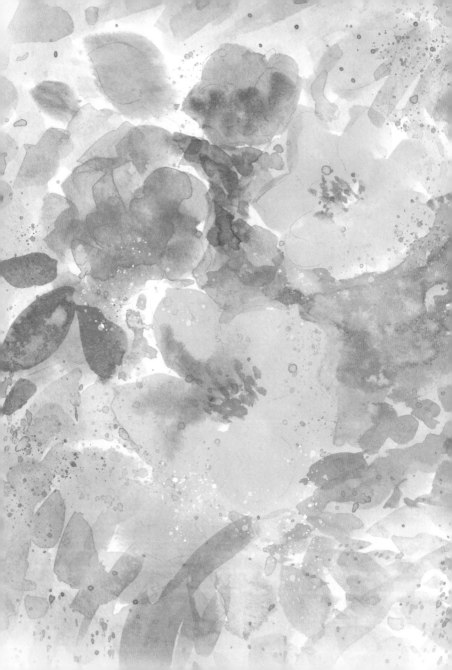

Summer

Peak Garden

Time is running out to find space for the plants I have yet to get into the soil. Every year, sometime in June, you can count on the following scene: me, standing, overwhelmed, amidst endless trays of seedlings. I started them indoors, many as far back as February. Back then, there was no grand plan, just some scrawled notes and the heightened enthusiasm that comes from being stuck indoors too long.

Sprinkled among a sea of plant babies are impulse buys that I had to have, but now I struggle, desperate for a place to put them. What goes into the garden now will determine what is reaped in the fall. There is an abundance of choice before me, but space in my urban lot is limited. I will not have another opportunity to grow some of these crops—this tomato variety, this new herb, this exciting flower—until next year. The pressure to choose well is enormous!

Summertime is the season of expansion. It is alive and energetic. There is a loud and raucous party in my garden that carries on all day, all the time. Everything in excess. New flowers and buds pop up quickly and burn out just as fast. The bees and pollinators come out to dance with their flowering partners in the sunshine and flit about in the heat. New species of bees, butterflies, and I don't even know what show up and join in. I am enriched and enlivened by new things to discover, taste, smell, and see. It's a wonderful time to be alive.

It is sometime around mid-June when the garden goes off-script. The seeds of plants I failed to cut back the previous fall sprout up in the hundreds, thousands. I lose count as I go from crouching, to kneeling, to sitting, to practically lying on the ground, plucking them out one by one by one. But I am a lousy editor. I want everyone to have a place, and so the garden transforms into a wild, free, and rebellious creature. And me, a frazzled parent chasing after my unruly plant children with pruners and a trowel. I won't catch up until fall.

This Flower Is Wilting

In hotter parts of the world, summer is an extreme, scorched-earth experience akin to a frozen northeastern winter in its severity. Plants go dormant in the heat, and the growing season sits on standby until fall rolls around to usher in another round of growth and abundance. For those of you gardening in these conditions, I suggest undertaking some of the projects in this chapter in late spring or early summer and flipping ahead to the winter chapter (excluding snow and ice activities) for further guidance.

Wherever you live, when the heat reaches a fever pitch, we all need some motivation to come out from the shade and go into our gardens. There are lots of fascinating things to discover if you can muster the energy. Go out and play! Just remember to bring a drink and wear a hat!

Stillness

Sit in a garden—any garden—after dark. If there are lights on, turn them off. Find somewhere comfortable to sit that puts you in the midst of it all. Bring an outdoor cushion, blanket, or chair if you need it. Be quiet and still. Wait for your eyes to adjust. Sit for 5 to 20 minutes as you listen to the sounds, smell the air, feel the ground beneath you, and take in the atmosphere of the nighttime garden.

Note: Bring a buddy with you if this pushes you outside your comfort zone or if the garden is located in a public place that feels unsafe.

o After you come in from this exercise, write about how it felt to sit in stillness in the garden, in the dark, at this time of day. Remember that this could be a positive or negative experience for many reasons. Don't feel obligated to see it either way. Write what was true for you.

Not all gardens are sanctuaries, even though we'd like them to be. (I once belonged to a community garden that was located off an alleyway. It was not a safe place to be after dark!) If there is no safe garden for you to visit in the evening, write about what you wish the experience could be and the feelings this provokes.

From Below

We often see our plants from high above, looking down. We hover over them as we go about our everyday chores—watering, weeding, plucking dead flowers. Have you ever looked at plants from below?

○ Lie down in a garden (or natural area) and look up at the plants towering above you. How does it feel to see the garden from this vantage point?

Land Art

My friend, Jen Lemen, teaches a course designed to help people create simple practices and daily rituals that cultivate connection and resilience during hard times. One of the practices she teaches is how to make small, contemplative "land artworks." Jen forages for fallen leaves, flower petals, and other bits from nature that hold some meaning for her, saving them until she is ready to create a piece of art that represents feelings and experiences that came up for her through the season. Because land art is transitional and not meant to last, it functions as a way of letting go and a reminder of the impermanence of life.

There are several kinds of land art, both traditional and contemporary. Many works are constructed in the form of a mandala, a Hindu and Buddhist symbol that represents the universe and the organization of life. While the word, loosely translated as "circle," is derived from ancient Sanskrit, the model itself is cross-cultural. Versions of it appear in medicine wheels, the yin-yang symbol, labyrinths, the Aztec calendar, and more.

As gardeners, working with plant materials in this way can be a creatively satisfying opportunity to track the changing seasons in your garden as well as to observe the diversity of life that resides there.

How to Make a Mandala

Collect a range of seasonal materials from your garden: bark, seeds, seed heads, stems, leaves, whole flowers, petals, flower buds, roots, or anything else you find.

Arrange the various bits in an artistic, circular, or spiral configuration on top of a uniform natural surface, such as grass, soil, or mulch. Consider hard surface backdrops too. For example, a large piece of colored paper, a wooden tabletop, or a stone path. Go public and assemble your mandala where people can see and interact with it—the sidewalk, your driveway, or your front yard.

Allow nature to degrade or destroy your mandala.

○ What story does your mandala tell about your garden and the season right now? Do the plants you chose and the assemblage you created say anything about you?

What Falls

Lay an old white bedsheet or a piece of paper underneath a plant, bush, or tree. Gently shake the plant. Observe everything that falls onto the sheet or paper and list or draw them if you wish.

Look for the following:

- **Insects:** Include their eggs, larvae, or feces. How many are there? Can you identify them? An insect field guide can help (see Resources on page 222).
- **Plant debris:** Twigs, bark, or leaves
- **Seeds:** Are they from this plant or were they from elsewhere and caught here?
- **Flowers:** What stage of development are they in?

Vacation Goggles

Whenever I visit a new place, my first instinct is to wander around aimlessly with my camera exploring the immediate outdoor space. Even when my lodgings are a cheap roadside motel in the middle of nowhere, I always seem to find something that captures my curiosity. When you're in a new place and wearing vacation goggles, every little thing becomes wonderful and exciting.

Spend an hour, an afternoon, or a weekend visiting your garden as a guest rather than as The Gardener. Try to see things through the eyes of a visitor experiencing them for the very first time.

○ Where does your gaze fall first? List everything you see within the first 5 minutes.

○ Which plants entice you to move in closer to touch or smell them?

○ Are there areas of the garden that feel more inviting than others?

Go Further

Bring along a book, beverage, or something else you might enjoy on vacation and experience the garden as a green oasis. Try to stay in "just visiting" mode as opposed to the judging gardener mode. Are you able to appreciate the garden on this level? Can you feel some renewed pride as the steward of this land?

Life in a Container

Potted plants are a lovely feature in gardens of all types and sizes. For many of us living in cities, our entire garden is made up of containers. There is nothing lesser about this type of garden—the only difference is scale. Amazingly, an entire ecosystem is held within even the smallest pot. The world inside it, while restrained, is a micro version of the larger world in terra firma.

In my gardening life, I have had all sorts of gardens and have treated each as living ecosystems. Given the number of critters that attempt to hitch a ride as I shift potted plants indoors each fall, I think it's fair to say that they sure don't know the difference between pots and beds. Containers can have nooks and crannies in which to hide, plant bits to eat, and flowers to pollinate. Give it some time and even the sterile "soilless mix" that comes in a bag will evolve into something that is fully alive with some of the microorganisms you find in the ground.

Looking at my potted plants in this way has given me a new appreciation of the complexity of the contained world and has helped me to strategize solutions for their care that I would not have thought of otherwise.

- Sit at a distance and watch your potted plant(s) for a few minutes. Do any insects pay a visit?
- Now get closer. Have any insects or critters taken up permanent residence? Try checking underneath the pot! Slugs, snails, and pill bugs often curl up inside drainage holes.
- Using your index finger, root around a little in the soil. Anything going on in there? Has the quality, texture, color, or content of the soil changed since it was first potted? Has the depth of the soil eroded?

Go Further

Check back on the same pot at the end of the growing season and repeat the activities just mentioned. How has the ecology of your potted garden changed over time?

Water Is Life

For many years, I grew gardens in difficult urban spaces that had no access to running water. Consequently, watering was an arduous chore, especially in high summer on a rooftop where thirsty plants in pots would dry out daily, or sometimes even faster!

I have access to an outdoor tap and hoses now, but I still do a lot of watering by hand. I sometimes resent the labor, especially during a heat wave, but most days I try to approach the task as a ritual, an opportunity to spend time with the plants and give back to them (see Reciprocity on page 178). Set in this context, water is an offering, and the act is a thank-you to the garden and all that it gives me. This mindset also keeps me conscious of the fact that water itself is something to be respected. It gives us all life. It is not limitless.

○ For the next 4 weeks, set this intention and create a ritual around the act of watering your plants (indoors and/or out). Write here if it changes your feelings about the task. (It's all right if you still hate it by the end!)

Leaf Shapes

Choose 3 to 5 leaves from your indoor or outdoor garden and draw their shapes. Trace the leaves if drawing intimidates you.

- Which shapes are most common in your garden?
- Leaf shape is a useful tool in plant identification. Try to find a leaf that represents each of the following shapes:

1 **Linear:** Longer than the width (e.g., grasses)
2 **Ovate:** Egg-shaped with broader base
3 **Spatulate:** Broad and rounded at the top with a narrow base
4 **Deltoid:** Triangular, often with rounded bottom corners
5 **Hastate:** Triangular, but elongated like a spearhead
6 **Elliptic:** An oval that is twice as long as it is wide

1   2   3   4   5   6

Herbarium

An herbarium is a collection of preserved plant materials, either whole (from root to tip) or parts, that is used to catalog the flora of an area.

○ Collect 20 different leaves and flowers from your garden, and press and dry them flat to preserve over the long term. (See instructions on the facing page.)

Don't feel obligated to get fancy about the plants you collect. Viola flowers and maple leaves are obvious choices, but what about carrot tops, tomato leaves, or your favorite hot pepper plant? Sometimes splendor in the garden can be found in unexpected places.

Quick Guide to Pressing Plants

I've owned several plant presses, and while they have their merits, the "press" I reach for most often is a heavy, oversize cookbook. Other old, hefty books, including dictionaries, catalogs, and phone books made of absorbent matte paper, work well too. Sandwich the leaves and flowers between pieces of newspaper or plain copy paper to help soak up moisture and prevent ink or dye from transferring between the plants and the book. Drying time varies between leaves and depends on your climate, but it can take days or weeks. Leave them until they are crisp. That's really all there is to it!

Make an Herbarium

Once dry, mount the plant parts into a scrapbook or artist sketchbook, or onto individual sheets of heavyweight and acid-free paper or card stock. There are special thin and sticky herbarium strips that you can buy online, but double-sided, acid-free tape is a more accessible option that won't yellow with age. Assemble loose sheets into a book format, such as a binder or folder, and include the name of the plant and the date it was collected. You could also use the sheets to create homemade greeting cards, or frame the pages and hang them on the wall.

Go Barefoot

Have you ever gone barefoot in your garden? I put my bare feet on the ground as a reminder that I too am a wild being that belongs to something bigger than myself: the plants and animals that live here, the land, the earth. We are all interconnected.

○ Take off your shoes and socks and allow the skin of your feet to touch a patch of grass, mulch, soil, or smooth stone, if you have it. If these options aren't available to you, stand wherever you are. Feel the texture of the earth beneath you. Can you feel how you are held by the solidness of the ground?

Sightless

Close your eyes or cover them with a blindfold and engage with the garden without this sense. Smell plants. Touch them. Touch the soil. Listen—what do you hear? Feel what is special about the garden without using eyesight to inform your perspective.

Tiny Aliens

All insects have their place and a role to perform. The health of the garden, if not our very lives, depends on them. Bees, butterflies, flies, ants, moths, and even some beetles pollinate our food crops, making them integral to plant reproduction. Pill bugs, millipedes, and slugs aid in the decay of dead foliage, and carnivorous insects, such as spiders, mantids, and ichneumon wasps, keep the population of vegetarian insects from exploding. We need insects as much as we might loathe some of them. And a balanced garden needs all kinds of insects—including the "bad guys."

Symbiotic relationships are everything in the garden. In that sense, it seems superficial or at least shortsighted to divide insects up into categories of good and bad, although, in all fairness, I can't blame you for harboring some resentment toward the aphids that have demolished your kale or the slugs that won't leave anything leafy and green well enough alone. When the balance tips out of our favor, invertebrates quickly lose their charm.

I'm convinced that if aliens have landed, they've been here among us all along, inhabiting tiny insect bodies and studying our strange human habits through the antenna eyes of slugs and snails. My first decent macro camera lens spawned a new pastime of stalking bumblebees and wasps around the garden, taking photos, and then blowing the images up really big on my computer screen. What I have found there is the stuff of far-out, low-budget movies and dystopian nightmares: freaky compound eyes, microscopic hairs, pointy fangs, and the most delicate, lace-like wings. I get chills (and thrills) every time.

The more I learn about these strange earth inhabitants, the cooler I think they are, even the creepy ones that make my whole body shudder. Over the years, I've developed a surprising pride of purpose in having created a garden that is hospitable to a diverse range of insect life. All are welcome. (Except maybe the lily beetles. Those guys are jerks.) Every new insect that lights upon the garden is an opportunity to learn something new about the world close to home and a way to reimagine my urban landscape as a place that can nurture an abundance of life rather than consume it. It's humbling to realize how many seemingly exotic beings there are quietly living right under my nose (and feet), unnoticed by my human eye. Knowing how many I have "discovered" by chance, it's mind-blowing to think about how many more I have yet to find. In that sense, the garden is an opportunity to satisfy wanderlust without ever leaving home.

Test Your Knowledge

○ Quickly, off the top of your head, list 5 insects that are commonly found in your region.

○ List 3 to 5 beneficial insects that you've seen in your garden. (If you're unsure whether or not they're beneficial to your garden, look them up online.) What role do they play in the garden?

○ List 3 to 5 problem insects that you've seen in your garden. (Anything that eats or damages your plants, like snails or aphids, might be considered problematic.) What positive role do they play in your garden's ecosystem?

Floral Forms

Comb your garden for as many examples as you can find of the following flower forms:

1   **Solitary:** The classic form; one flower on a stem, separate from others

2   **Corymb:** Outermost flowers are on longer stems than the innermost, so all flowers are on the same level

3   **Spike:** Flowers develop off main stem

4   **Umbel:** Shaped like an umbrella turned inside out

5   **Catkin:** Flowers develop from main stem without stalks, like a spike, but there are no petals (such as willow and birch)

6   **Capitulum:** Many separate flowers (without stalks) clustered close together (such as the center of a daisy)

7   **Raceme:** Like a spike, but flowers have their own small stems, called pedicels

8   **Panicle:** Like a raceme, but each stem has more than one flower

1

2

3

4

5

6

7

8

Free Plants

Grow a cutting gleaned from someone else's garden. It can be from a friend or a stranger. Ask for permission, and respect the parent plant by making a clean, careful cut.

How to Make a Cutting

1   Snip a 4- to 6-inch (10- to 15-cm) stem on an angle, just above a node (the juncture on the stem where leaves are attached). Be sure that there is at least 1 other node on the stem that you cut. More is preferred.

2   Pluck off 1 to 2 sets of leaves from the bottom until there are 1 to 2 inches (2.5 to 5 cm) of bare stem. Remove any flowers or buds that have formed on the cutting.

3   Stick the bare stem(s) in a small jar of water and place in a sunny but protected spot. At least 1 node should always be submerged in the water since this is where the roots will form. To root in soil, repeat these steps, but push the cut end of the stem into a pot filled with well-draining potting soil.

4   Keep the jar topped up with water or the soil evenly moist until the cuttings have formed a healthy root system. If propagating in water, plant in soil once roots have developed.

- **If you got your cutting from a friend:** Does a plant that comes from a friend carry special meaning? Are you more likely to work harder to maintain its health than that of other plants in your indoor or outdoor garden?
- **If you got your cutting from a stranger:** Does a plant gleaned from a complete stranger's garden carry any meaning for you? Is there still something about it that is different from a plant that you bought?

I think I am
the garden's
mother, but
in truth,
she is mine.

Moth Movie

Before nightfall, hang an old white bedsheet against a wall or fence to create a movie screen of sorts. If you don't have a flat surface to work with, tie a long piece of cord to each of the top corners of the sheet and secure the ends around trees, metal posts, or tall bamboo stakes sunk into the soil. Shine a strong outdoor lamp or flashlight onto the sheet and wait. Any type of light will attract moths, although mercury vapor and black lights work best.

○ Can you identify the moths? (A field guide can help. See Resources on page 222.)

○ Draw, paint, or photograph them, if you'd like.

○ Do any other insects make a guest appearance?

.

Bird's-Eye View

Set up a ladder or sturdy chair in the center of the garden (or as close as you can get to the center). Get help holding it. Stay safe! Climb up with a camera and take pictures or shoot a 360-degree video from that vantage point.

○ What do you see from here that you didn't notice before?

○ How does this vantage point change your perspective on the overall garden or certain parts of it?

Taste Something New

Sample a part of an edible plant that you have never tried before. (Before sampling, ensure the plant is safe to eat. Wash it, particularly if it was in the ground, such as a root system. If you're prone to allergies, sample small quantities first.)

○ Write about each of the plants you try, describing the flavors that come up.

Some ideas to try:
- Basil flowers
- Black currant leaf
- Carrot greens
- Dandelion petal
- Garlic scapes (flower)
- Green, immature coriander seed
- Horseradish leaf
- Lovage root or seeds
- Nasturtium seed pod or flower (focus just on the spur or bottom portion of the flower)
- Rose petal or hips (fruit)
- Sage blossom
- Turnip tops
- Young radish seed pods
- Zucchini flower

Last Days of Summer

Watch for these signs and check them off:

☐ Cooler days and nights

☐ Shorter days

☐ Trilling cicadas (depending on your location)

☐ Tree leaves changing color and even dropping

☐ Less fruit appearing on early tomato varieties

☐ Apples and other early fall fruit beginning to ripen

☐ A second round of cool-season plants appearing, such as mustard greens, lettuce, or dandelion

☐ Field plants in the grasses and sunflower families beginning to flower with abandon

☐ Garlic stalks shifting from green to yellow or brown

○ Write down any other signs that you have noticed. Depending on your climate, you may find that certain crops are ready for harvest or have finished producing, specific flowering perennials are done or just taking off, or that space has opened up in the beds for new seedlings to emerge.

Additional Notes from Summer

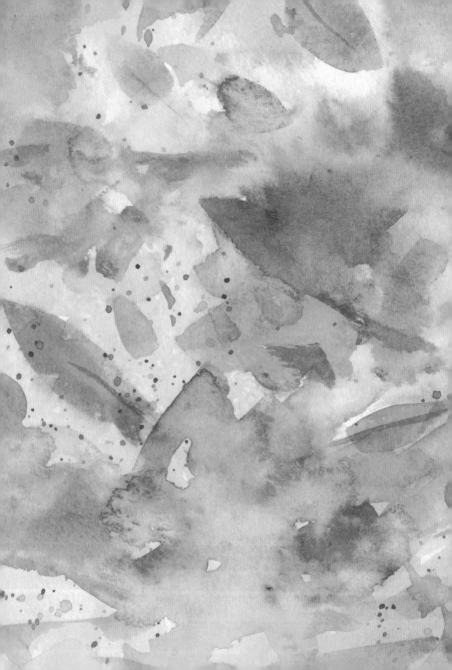

Fall

Let Go

I love the fall. The crisp air, the sweet smell of rot. The warm autumnal color palette. The remembrance of childhood in a pile of fallen leaves. After months of sweaty heat, the cooler air is a welcome relief that reinvigorates me as well as the plants in the garden. That's a good thing because there is work to be done: moving pots and planting, collecting seeds for next year, tucking in annual beds, and so much more. Fall is busy, but it is also a time for celebration: a chance to enjoy the fruits of our labor, bask in the bounty of the harvest, and appreciate the year's gardening triumphs.

In the fall, there is something about the way some plants and trees burst with one last dramatic display of color and then drop their leaves in a climactic swoosh, telling us that letting go doesn't have to be sad; it can also be a spectacular event. However, if you live in a cold climate as I do, winter is always looming somewhere in the future. Many people appreciate the coming season of ice and cold; I can't say I'm among them. I can mentally and physically prepare myself for winter's arrival, but I can't change it or stop it. It is the reason why, despite so many fond feelings, I also anticipate autumn with some trepidation.

Perhaps one of gardening's greatest lessons is tucked somewhere inside both our resistance to and acceptance of these cycles and rhythms that we can't sway to suit our bidding. The growing season will come to a close; the garden will become a scene of dormancy, death, and decay. If we learn to let go, even a little, growing a garden can offer preparation for the inevitability of life's greatest darkness: loss and death. Winter always comes.

Like everyone, I have lost a lot to death, and as I age I have feared my own mortality and the inevitable loss of loved ones still here with me. In the garden and in life, I've allowed my anxieties about what comes next to stand in the way of being fully open to what is here now. All this gorgeous autumnal splendor surrounds me, yet I waste so much time dreading the coming snow!

It is to the garden that I am looking to find another way to live. There is something old and complicated in the evolutionary relationship between plants and people. Plants are like us. We see ourselves in them. It's no wonder that so many metaphors for life relate to their anatomy and processes. The perennials in my garden elegantly demonstrate how to transform. They show me how to let go of the old in order to make way for winter's rest and spring's eventual renewal. I want to be like them and use the fall season to release old baggage and wounds, so that I can sit quietly in patience through the winter while I wait for the promise of spring's return.

Be with the garden as it is now. Look to the brilliance and wisdom of the trees. Trust that spring will come again. Let go.

Taking Stock

Fall is the season of release and an invitation to practice letting go. After twenty-odd autumns as a gardener, however, I'm still not very good at it. As the first frost date approaches, I always end up frantically bringing in more plants than I planned for or can reasonably house. Each year on the night of the killing frost, I go to bed unsettled, thinking about those who were left behind. The next thing I know I'm outside in my pajamas dragging potted plants into the kitchen. I just can't bear to see a plant die! Inevitably, in overcrowded conditions, the plants I sought to rescue slowly expire anyway. I'm an experienced gardener. I know how this story will play out. Yet the next fall is always a rerun of the same sitcom.

Use the theme of letting go to take stock of your garden.

- Are there plants that didn't thrive in the space provided or work aesthetically that you can purge to make room for something new?
- Why do you think it is time to let go of these plants?
- Is there anything holding you back from letting go?

Slowly, Carefully

In her book, *The Sound of a Wild Snail Eating*, author Elisabeth Tova Bailey, bedridden due to chronic illness, recounts her meditations on a small snail that has hitched a ride in a potted violet next to her nightstand. Despite her confinement, Elisabeth finds a way to connect with nature through quietly watching the snail's slow life. Along the way, she makes many astute observations about this small creature that ultimately relate back to her own slowed-down life.

Late fall is generally a time of seasonal ailments and a slowing down of life in and out of the garden. Use Elisabeth's example and bring the garden to you. This is a simple activity that you can do whether or not you find yourself confined to your bed for any length of time.

○ Place a potted plant or vase of plant materials (sticks, a cutting, flowers) at your bedside or in a quiet corner of your home. Sit or lay down next to it for 5 minutes each day. Jot down anything you notice, no matter how small or seemingly unimportant. Sketch it if you prefer.

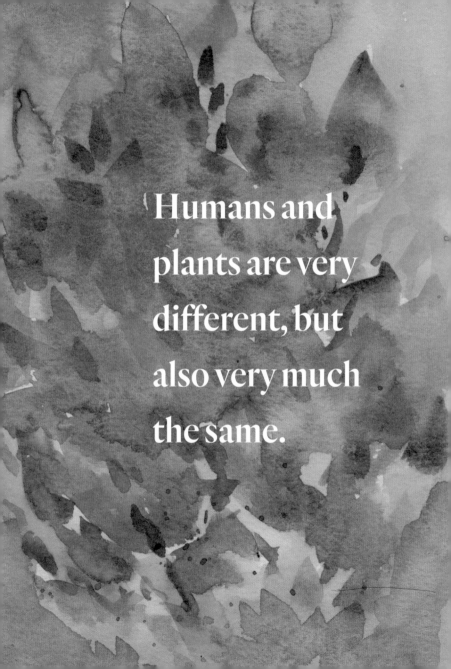

Humans and plants are very different, but also very much the same.

Stems

As you work in the garden, look closely at the stems of each plant. Stem shapes are one way of quickly identifying plants—particularly those of the same family—and a detail that we tend to overlook. For example, many plants of the mint family (*Lamiaceae*) have square stems.

○ <u>Stem Shape:</u> Can you find square stems? Round stems? Oval? Hollow? Flattened?

○ <u>Stem Features:</u> Look for stems that are hairy, smooth, or thorny.

Have you noticed a correlation between plants with the same stem shape?

Difference/Sameness

Collect 6 leaves from the same plant. Choose leaves from different areas of growth: top of the plant, new growth, mature growth, and so on.

Lay them all out together. How similar are they? Are there any notable differences in shape, size, color, pattern, texture?

- What do you think accounts for these differences?
- Are some leaves healthier than others?
- Did the leaves develop at different times when the temperature or climate conditions varied? Other weather patterns to consider include heavy rainfall, drought, a snap freeze, or a heat wave.
- Were some of the leaves attacked by insects or disease?

Go Further

Find 6 flowers, fruits, seed pods, seeds, or similar from the same plant and repeat this activity with each part.

Growing into Awareness

David Holmgren, one of the co-originators of permaculture (a holistic system of agriculture whose roots lie in Indigenous practices), says that the best lessons are learned through "contemplative awareness," a sort of nondoing that can only happen when we give considerable time and space to our curiosities. This kind of skill is one that can be honed, but it's unachievable if we are always goal-oriented and in a rush.

Giving ourselves permission to slow down, observe, reflect, and stop working can feel childish, if not inconvenient, given the demands of adult life. Many of us see the act of gardening as a playful respite or hobby; taking time to stop and observe the garden without "working the garden" borders on selfish luxury. ("I could be—no, I should be—weeding right now! Or sowing seeds. Or harvesting the radishes.") While there is something to be said for the way these repetitive tasks lead us into a meditative state and clear our mind for new ideas, there are also benefits to making time to look closely, sit still, or literally smell the roses.

○ Take a moment to jump back to the front of this book and do the activity called Begin Here on page 17. Walk through your garden and mindfully, intentionally observe. What has changed since the last time you did this exercise?

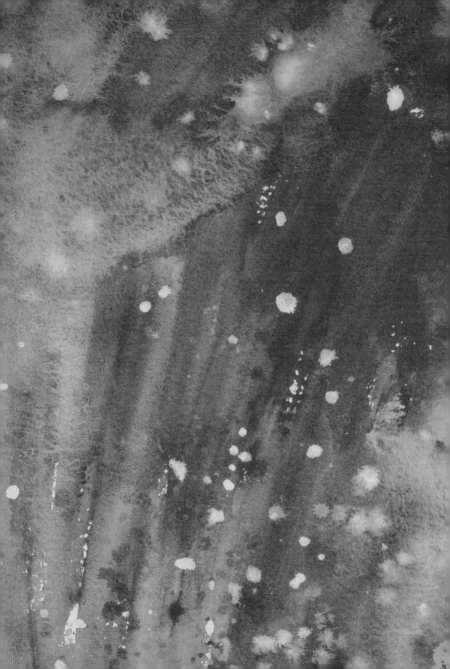

Play in Your Garden

In her workbook for writers, *What It Is*, artist Lynda Barry explains that as adults we have a misunderstanding of play as a state of ease, when, for children, it can be very serious business, a way to work through life's challenges and find a path toward understanding and growth.

Gardening is a kind of deep, serious play that works on our minds and reconnects us to ourselves. It is an enriching, experiential activity and a place to search for and find meaning. When we engage with the garden as pure work without allowing ourselves the space to play, we potentially cut ourselves off from new pathways to knowledge and creative solutions to challenges both in life and in the garden. Being playful in the garden ultimately makes us better gardeners!

o   How do you think gardening as play has contributed to learning within the garden?

o   How has it contributed to learning and/or finding solutions to problems outside the garden?

The Shape of Things

Look at a plant or flower, and, in your mind, try to reduce it to its basic shapes. For example, when I look at tulips and some daffodils, I see triangles. A daisy or sunflower is a circle with ovals surrounding it. Lots of plant stems seem to be comprised of a line with several ovals (leaves) along each side.

○ Use this basic premise to make simple drawings of plants and flowers in your garden.

○ Which shapes appear most frequently?

○ Are there combinations of shapes that complement each other? What about combinations that clash?

Bird Spotting

Write down the names of every bird spotted in your garden. If you do not know their names, simply sketch or describe a few notable characteristics (color, body shape, beak shape, what they are eating) so you can look them up later.

Note: If you do not have a garden that birds visit, do this exercise elsewhere, such as in a public park.

Value Scale

Collect as many leaves as you can in different shades of the same color—for example, all green or all red. Arrange them in a line, circle, or spiral from lightest to darkest, or vice versa.

Take a photo if you wish, or press and affix to paper to create a permanent artwork (see Herbarium on page 106).

Go Further

Repeat with other colors and other plant parts, such as petals and fruit.

Seeds on the Move

If you've ever watched a maple key (a type of seed pod) spiral down to the ground, then you're already familiar with seeds that exploit the power of the wind to transport their genetic material to far-flung reaches.

Not all breeze-blown seeds have wings and whirl like a helicopter. Tumbleweed also uses the wind to get around. Others have a parachute-like design, such as milkweed, salsify, and dandelion. Still others, like fountain grass, have a light, feathery form that can also be picked up in a gust of wind.

Explosive dehiscence is another seed dispersal method in which pods that are fully ripe split open and fling their seeds outward. Plants that utilize this method include jewelweed, dwarf mistletoe, violet, geranium, and phlox.

- Can you find examples of either of these seed dispersal methods (wind blown or explosive dehiscence) in your garden?
- What are some other seed dispersal methods that you notice (or have noticed) in the garden or the outside world?

Zoom In

Collect an assortment of plant bits from your walks or from your garden. Look at them closely using a magnifying glass. Take photos with a macro lens or macro setting on your camera or phone if that is available to you.

○ Write down and/or sketch any details you are able to observe with magnification that could not be seen with your own eyes.

10 Minutes of Work

Let's say you have just 10 minutes to garden today.

○ What will you do? What do you think you should do? What do you
want to do? How do you prioritize need over desire? Now, set a
timer for 10 minutes and step into the garden.

○ When you return, consider the following: How did what you
thought you would do compare with what you actually did? Do
you wish you had done something different?

The Chosen One

Choose a plant in your garden (indoor and greenhouse plants also count), and when you're ready, set a timer for 10 minutes. Observe every minute detail that you can about that plant. Write it all down here.

Colorful Roots

Perhaps it is because roots reside underneath the ground, but unless they're grown for food, they are an oft-overlooked part of the plant "body."

As you're digging up, moving around, and planting new crops, trees, bushes, and perennials this fall, take note of plants that have colorful roots.

A few plants to look for:

- Beet
- Bloodroot (*Sanguinaria*)
- California poppy (*Eschscholzia californica*)
- Carrot
- Goldenseal (*Hydrastis canadensis*)
- Madder (*Rubia tinctorum*)
- Meadow rue (*Thalictrum*)
- Plume poppy (*Macleaya cordata*)
- Radish
- Red root (*Ceanothus americanus*)
- Sweet potato
- Yellow dock (*Rumex crispus*)

The Spider Game

After dark, hold a flashlight against your forehead (almost between your eyes) and shine the beam into the garden. Be sure to look down low around grassy areas and plant stalks. Spider eyes often reflect the light. Scan for little sparks or glows, sort of like tiny bike reflectors. If you follow the reflection, you will almost always find a spider.

Angry Gardening

Most gardeners know that gardening isn't all peace and love and good vibes. For better or worse, we bring ourselves and the world into the garden with us. Sometimes what we need from our time there isn't beautiful living things to contemplate and a place to slow down and unwind. Sometimes what we need is pure, raw catharsis.

I have, on occasion, entered the garden absolutely fuming over an especially enraging personal conflict or something awful that I read in the news. This is when I turn to the most physical and aggressive activities available: working the compost, moving plants, pruning thick branches, or digging out pernicious weeds. There have been times when I've caught myself not just digging but jabbing at the soil, not pruning the raspberry canes so much as beheading them. It feels good to blow off some steam and get it all out.

Working the garden is an effective therapy for untangling the most complex and difficult emotions, and a safe place to confront and release unwanted energy from our bodies. Somehow, the earth seems to absorb it. The garden doesn't judge. Occasionally, what troubles me is no match for a dose of physical movement and the happy-making, mood-altering microbes that live in the soil. On other occasions, the troubles are still there, but I get a sense of clarity and release from the experience that leaves me better equipped to deal with them and move forward.

○ The next time you're having a bad day, head to the garden, even if all you can fit in is 5 or 10 minutes. How do you feel afterward? Which activities felt the most cathartic?

Jack Frost

The first hard or killing frost can be devastating to a gardener. Here in Toronto, I start checking the forecast religiously as soon as October hits. I always know when it is coming, but I am never truly ready. No matter how many years I have been doing this, the emotions are the same.

As I step outdoors the morning after to take a mental head count of the fallen, I am overcome with a sense of loss. Goodbye, fresh tomato leaf smell. Goodbye, gorgeous new basil. Goodbye, really rad but ultimately random plant I couldn't find space for indoors. The feeling is sort of like saying goodbye to a visiting friend when you know it will be ages before you'll see one another again.

That said, just as nature takes our garden away, it graces us with a few fleeting moments of stunning, otherworldly beauty. It sweeps through in the night like a giant, sparkling paintbrush, and what is left behind is magical, but fleeting. Don't miss it. There is so much there to explore with your eyes and document with pen and paper or a camera.

After the first frost, take some time for the following:

- Get up close and look at individual crystals of ice on leaves. Use a magnifying glass or a camera with macro ability.

- If you have a camera, take photos of everything that catches your eye. Close-up shots work best to really capture the magic of frost-kissed leaves, foliage, and fruit. (The reflective quality of the frost can mess up your camera's metering, and I suggest bouncing more light into the shot with a piece of white cardstock or switching your settings to slightly "overexpose" the image.) Move around your plants. Shoot from overhead or from below. To create a glimmery effect, pick a position that allows sun to come into the frame from the side.

- Explore ways that the frost enhances the structures of plants. For example, frost that has collected along a leaf's margins highlights its shape. It can also make veining pop.
- Look for frost that has collected on spiderwebs, glass, and inert objects.
- Take note of which parts of the garden were hit hardest by frost. Were any completely untouched? What conditions in your garden could account for these differences? How can you make use of the protected spots within the space?
- After the frost has melted, go back and check on your plants. Make a list of the ones that made it and those that didn't. Don't forget to fill in the date (see page 168). On a practical level, I often return to my own record of annual frosts to determine what can be left outside and what should come indoors or be harvested before future frosts.
- What type of damage has been done to specific plants? I find that some skeletonize and others turn to mush almost immediately. Others drop their leaves, wilt, or blacken. Which plants rebound?

First Frost Date

Last Days of Fall

Watch for these signs and check them off below:

☐ Cooler days and nights

☐ Shorter and darker days

☐ Fewer insects and pollinators; activity slowing down

☐ Fewer plants flowering

☐ The leaves of trees and other plants changing color and/or dropping

☐ Productivity declining on late tomato varieties

☐ Frost on plants in the early morning

☐ Changing color palette of the garden (often toward yellow and brown)

☐ Perennials beginning to wind down, change color, or die back entirely. In some climates, the opposite may occur as cool-season plants take on a new life.

○ Write down any other signs that you have noticed. Depending on your climate, you may find that certain crops are ready for harvest or have finished producing; specific flowering perennials may be done or just taking off; or space has opened up in the beds for new seedlings to emerge.

Additional Notes from Fall

Winter

Slow Down

Winter is a season of stasis. Rest. When the weather is extreme, the natural inclination for all living things is to slow down—humans included. The body needs to conserve energy under stress. It wants to find a cozy spot and settle in. It craves rest and rejuvenation. I can feel my own body following suit as days shorten and the cold comes on. I am like the trees and the herbaceous perennials as they pull back and sink their energy underneath the ground. Humans and plants are very different, but also very much the same.

But in our industrialized world, our bodies and minds have been trained to disregard the natural rhythms of nature—our nature—and are instead encouraged to maintain an impossible, relentless pace. Stay busy. Keep producing.

I used to fall in step with this directive (still do sometimes), pushing my body and ignoring its needs. I suspect that, unconsciously, this is one reason why I've been so averse to the winter months. I didn't want to slow down. Didn't want to be brought into the earth's quiet movements. To give myself over to the ebb and flow of the seasons and their profound effect on my body made me feel too vulnerable, not in control. Too animal.

It could be that what is behind our culture's race against rest is more than just a social pressure to outperform. Perhaps, deep down, we are scared. There are obvious associations between the cycle of life and the cycles of the year. It's even in our language. If spring is the season of birth, light, and plenty, then winter is its antithesis: death, darkness, and hardship. Maybe if we keep going and control the pace, we can avoid it altogether. Or at least avoid feeling it.

As I age, I have learned that there is something to be gained in the stillness of winter, in respecting a season of rest before the hustle and bustle of spring. To be honest, my body came to this conclusion without me! It demands that, like it or not, I get in sync with its needs. I feel each seasonal shift intensely now and am susceptible to its extremes, or, rather, I am aware of my susceptibility. For I was always vulnerable. The only difference now is awareness and acknowledgment.

It turns out that vulnerability is not such a bad thing. It's honest and very human. The reality of being alive is that it ends in death. Trying to outrun it or avoid feeling the depth of it doesn't make it any less inevitable. Instead, it disconnects us from our wholeness, our connection to each other, and to a deeper belonging to everything else. The plants, the earth, the creatures around us, you, and me.

Reciprocity

Like many gardeners, I started out making gardens based on what they could do for me. Unconsciously, I told myself, "I made this, therefore it is mine. I grow and take what I want." I have never owned a house or land, and for a long time my primary garden wasn't even in the ground, yet the language of ownership, control, and extraction lay at the foundation of my relationship to those spaces.

I strived to be a good steward and respect the environment in my practices, but fundamentally, I still saw the garden as a pyramid where I stood at the top. Because I was the creator and my labor and resources went into building the garden, everything that happened there placed me at the center and was, for better and for worse, under my control.

In her book, *Braiding Sweetgrass: Indigenous Wisdom, Scientific Knowledge, and the Teachings of Plants*, botanist Robin Wall Kimmerer writes that we are currently suffering from "species loneliness," a deep estrangement from the natural world. We are lonely for authentic engagement with each other and disconnected from our place in nature. In placing ourselves at the top of a hierarchy, we don't recognize relatedness or kinship to other beings besides our own.

In many Indigenous cultures, plants, animals, fungi, and all other parts of nature are considered our relatives. Everything in the natural world is alive and has a personhood. In the English language, we use the pronoun "it" to address anything that is not human. While we may only use "it" as a figure of speech, Wall Kimmerer makes the argument that the language sets us aside from nature, opening the door for the sort of exploitation that has led us to this critical moment in the earth's history. Without kinship, we are absolved of moral responsibility.

Reciprocity, on the other hand, is all about relationship. It acknowledges that we are all connected—plants, soil, water, creatures, us—there is no pyramid or center. We share a mutual responsibility in taking care of one another. As I tend the garden, the garden tends to me.

It's easy enough to make the shift toward mutual care and responsibility. Some basic ways to give back to the garden are at the heart of everyday practices. For example, making compost is a way of honoring the web of life: putting back what is taken out. Fertilizing is referred to as "feeding," a form of nourishment that can be extractive or replenishing depending on what we use as fertilizer. Pruning can be a way to keep plants small and contained, but it can also help plants grow healthy and more resilient. So much of this comes down to how we apply these methods and who they serve.

○ What are some other everyday practices you're already doing that are forms of giving back?

○ What are some things you can do (practices and rituals) that can help shift your relationship with the garden away from hierarchical thinking where you are located at the top?

I thought I
was learning
about plants;
it turns out
I was really
learning
about myself.

Belonging

As we discussed in Reciprocity on page 178, the language we use isn't just a reflection of our reality; it often defines it. "Belonging" can signify ownership or a relationship—two closely tied but divergent meanings. It's become a habit for many of us to think of the spaces we garden as property, one of a list of things that belong to us. But we won't be here forever; the land will. How you choose to use even the tiniest parcel matters.

What if rather than saying, "The garden belongs to me," you said, "I belong to the garden"?

o How does that wording change your perspective?

o How does belonging to the garden as a relationship of mutual care feel inside your body?

Fantasy Wish List

When I was a kid, the arrival of catalogs from Sears and Consumers Distributing carried the same excitement that seed catalogs do as an adult today. Back then, I didn't have the money or agency to make purchases, yet I felt the same thrill of anticipation due, at least in part, to a game we played that I'll call Fantasy Wish Fulfillment. The object of the game was to go through the entire catalog without skipping any pages and choose an item from each page. Being a kid, the real fun started in the toy section.

○ Choose a seed catalog and play the gardener's version of the Fantasy Wish Fulfillment game. Flip through, page-by-page, and make a selection from each page or spread based entirely on desire. Set aside all practicalities of the real world and imagine a fantasy scenario in which you have unlimited space and money, and the growing conditions are always, magically, ideal. Set a time limit per page if that helps. List your fantasy choices on these pages.

○ Which sections did you slog through and which ones made your heart race with possibility?

○ Did your fantasy choices reveal any previously unknown desires? Will you grow any of these plants?

○ Did you notice a trend in your choices? For example, more inedible plants than usual; bigger plants; specific groups, such as succulents, medicinal plants, or dye plants?

Go Further

Save this catalog and come back to it in a year. Go through the same exercise. Did your choices differ this time around or did you choose many of the same things?

It Lives

We tend to think of winter as an ending. In many parts of the world, gardening activities come to a halt. Yet if you look closely enough, you will find green things that are still alive, even in places that experience a deep freeze. They're there; sometimes you just have to dig around for them underneath a layer of dead leaves or snow.

○ Explore your winter garden in search of moss, lichen, living leaves, and buds. List or draw them on the following pages.

From Memory

Relying on memory, set a timer for 5 minutes and quickly jot down everything that you know or have observed about a plant that you grow in your garden. Any little detail counts, from the smell, to the color of the leaves, to its peak season. Try to choose a plant from the garden that is currently dormant or no longer alive, or a houseplant that is not in the room with you.

○   Are you surprised by how much or how little you can recall?

○   Now, set the timer for 10 to 15 minutes and sketch the plant from memory.

Go Further

Repeat this activity with other plants, insects, birds, lizards, toads, or other living beings that are a part of or a visitor to your garden.

A Room with a View

Set up a comfortable place in front of a window that looks out onto the garden and spend some cozy time there quietly observing its goings-on. Write down the little things that come to your attention. Do this daily, weekly, or monthly.

Windows are a literal and metaphorical way of framing the world or, in this case, the world that is your garden. Gazing upon the garden from the same place offers a certain consistency that can make it easier to see and take note of changes as they occur. If a window is not available, stand in the same spot in your garden and use an actual frame with the glass removed as a consistent shape through which to observe the garden from "outside." Hold it up in the same place each time and limit your observations to only what can be seen from within the frame.

Take note of the following:
- The overall color of the garden today; describe it in words or sketch it with colored pencils or pens
- Plants that are still green
- Plants that have left behind some point of interest (seed heads, stalks)
- Plants that have completely disappeared
- Garden visitors (birds, flying insects, mammals)
- Animal tracks and pathways in snow or mud
- Trees, bushes, or plants that are coming back or budding
- Plants that are blooming (warmer climates or other seasons)

Imperfection and Decay

We tend to prefer plants when they are freshly blooming and in their prime. As a photographer, I am not alone in plucking withered flowers and leaves from the frame to get the perfect, clean shot.

Why do we revile flowers and plants that are no longer perfect? Is there a different sort of beauty there that we are missing in our pursuit of the youthfulness of a new bud, a freshly opened bloom, or an unblemished leaf?

Years ago, while out on a winter walk with my camera in tow, I happened upon a community garden with open gates. Some of the plots had been cleaned up thoroughly, but there remained a few forgotten remnants of the summer garden season: a shriveled eggplant hanging like a pendant from the leafless stalk of a dead plant, seed pods with snowy caps, the tall skeletons of giant sunflowers. I found myself taken in by the beauty of these less-than-perfect specimens and began to seek them out in other gardens I visited no matter the time of year.

- Look for withering, old, or dying flowers, produce, and plants in your garden or any other garden you visit. Survey for leaves that have been pocked or deformed by insect and slug predation.
- Are there aspects of these blemished parts that you can appreciate aesthetically?
- Take photos and/or sketch them on the following pages.

Identify Seeds

Learning to identify plants as seeds is a great help if you happen to find a mix of random seeds in your pocket or the bottom of your seed-saving bin. I always do!

○ Choose a handful of seeds that you plan to grow this year and sketch them here. Make your drawings as simple or detailed as you like. Use paint, pencils, crayons, colored pens, or markers. Label each with the common name, Latin name, and cultivar if you know them.

Go Further

Look closely at each seed with a magnifying glass. Are any new details revealed with magnification?

Body of Knowledge

By habit, I touch and smell almost every plant I meet. Sometimes it gets me into trouble, and I've learned to be more mindful before sticking my nose into a new flower.

I used to think of these involuntary actions as personal quirks—just me being weirdo me. However, I've recently come to realize that touching and smelling the same plants thousands of times is a tactile, somatic (bodily) way of learning that has enhanced the intellectual knowledge I've accumulated in my years as a gardener. I'm better off for it.

Engaging our five senses is a different way of understanding, a form of inquiry that we hold in our body's memory, especially when the interaction is particularly potent. It's also communication, a way for plants to tell us about themselves. If I accidentally brush up against stinging nettle at peak season, that strange, almost electric pain that shoots through my nervous system is the plant's way of letting me know, loud and clear, to mind its boundaries. Believe me, I listen.

○ Where in your body do you know about plants?

○ What are some ways that you learn about plants somatically?

Garden Report

Take a photo of your garden every day, every week, or every month from the same position. Try to frame each image as closely to the original as possible. You can do this through a window inside your dwelling or from outdoors.

I have been doing this for years from the same upstairs window of my home. It has become an invaluable record of my garden as it changes through the years and the seasons. It's always surprising to look back and see the dramatic transformation from growth to decay that happens over a year.

Go Further

At the end of the first year, print out and assemble all your photos into a scrapbook (affix them in the same position on each page to make a flip-book).

Alternatively, post each image to your preferred social media platform as you go, and tag the images #[yourname]garden so you can access them all at once. You could also try making a time-lapse video with them using a free program, such as Time Lapse Assembler.

Elder Plants

"Elder" is a status I give to beloved plants that for one reason or another have garnered my respect. Usually they are food or medicinal plants. Sometimes they are weeds. I think of elders as friends, allies, mothers, and wise beings, and I miss them when their season ends. There was Elder Radish, a long-lived root that grew to a surprising size; also, Elder Dandelion, a huge colony of dandelion plants that lived at the edge of a pathway for several seasons.

Every year, around late winter, I find myself writing tributes to these esteemed plants as I await spring's return.

○ Are there plants like this in your garden or in a nearby field, park, forest, or other cultivated or wild space? Write a tribute to one of them.

Dead Stalks

In cold climates where winter is a season of quiet dormancy, it is often dead stalks and seed heads that provide the most visual interest. This can also be true in places with long periods of drought. Dead plants are not as easy to identify as living ones, but it is still a way of getting to know a plant out of season.

○ Can you identify the plants in your garden by their dried winter stalks? Sketch one here.

Note: The book *Weeds and Wildflowers in Winter* by Lauren Brown is an excellent resource for identifying winter's skeletal remains.

What Remains

When winter approaches its end and spring is just over the horizon, look around the garden and observe:

- What remains of the brown plant parts and seed stalks that were left behind at the end of the growing season?
- Have the seeds been stripped off?
- What condition are they in compared to the fall? Have they begun to disintegrate or decay?
- Have the colors changed?
- Have the stems fallen over?
- Were they consumed by critters or worn away by the elements?
- What about the roots of tender annuals? Did they begin to decompose in place?

Last Days of Winter

Watch for these signs and check them off:

- [ ] Warmer days and nights

- [ ] Longer days

- [ ] More active birds and other creatures

- [ ] Melting snow

- [ ] Soil warming up

- [ ] New growth emerging from the soil and on trees and shrubs

- [ ] Flowering bulbs and woodland blooms appearing

- [ ] The overall palette of the garden changing from white (snowy locations) or brown/yellow (warmer climates) to green

○ Write down any other signs you have noticed. In warmer climates, you may find that specific crops are ready for harvest or have finished producing, specific flowering perennials may be done or just taking off, or space is filling up in the beds as new seedlings emerge.

Additional Notes from Winter

End Here

In gardening, as is sometimes the case elsewhere in life, there are no endings, only cycles. Do this activity when you feel you have finished working with this book.

As with the Begin Here activity at the start of the journal, spend 5 to 10 minutes (or more) being with your garden. Quietly sit or stand, or slowly meander its paths. Pay attention, focusing on what you experience with your senses. Try to turn off judgments, such as what needs work, and the impulse to fret or fix things.

- Directly afterward, write down everything you can remember about what you experienced and observed.
- How did it feel in your body and mind to let go in this way now that you're more practiced in slowing down?

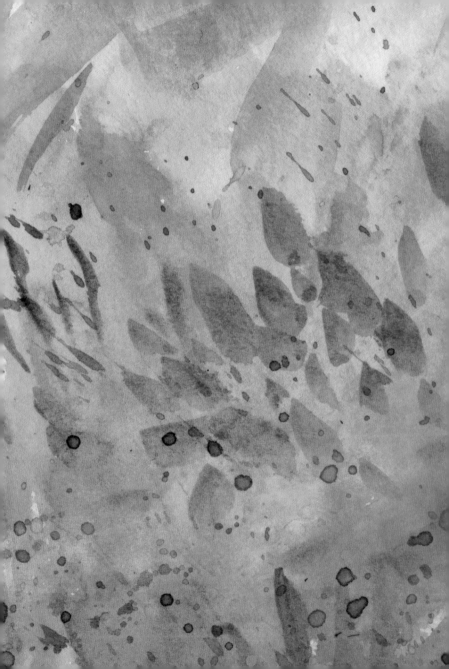

Gardening Is Resistance

Today and every day . . .
Grow and eat good food.
Find your grounding in the earth and
connect to the nature that is in you—
the nature that is you.
Make space for wildness. BE wild.
Tend and be tender.
Don't be good; be defiant.
Cultivate compassion and empathy.
Hold yourself in strength and dignity.
Hold each other.

Resources

Flora ID Guides

- Brill, Steve, and Evelyn Dean. *Identifying and Harvesting Edible and Medicinal Plants in Wild (and Not So Wild) Places*. New York: Harper Collins, 1994.

- INaturalist app, inaturalist.org

- Kallas, John. *Edible Wild Plants: Wild Foods from Dirt to Plate*. Layton, UT: Gibbs Smith, 2010.

- Mitchell, Alan. *Trees of North America*. London: Collins & Brown, 1987.

- Phillips, Roger. *Wild Food*. Boston: Little Brown and Company, 1986.

Fauna ID Guides

- Beletsky, Les. *Birds of the World*. Baltimore: Johns Hopkins University Press, 2006.

- Burris, Judy, and Wayne Richards. *The Life Cycles of Butterflies: From Egg to Maturity, a Visual Guide to 23 Common Garden Butterflies*. North Adams, MA: Storey Publishing, 2007.

- Merlin Bird ID App, merlin.allaboutbirds.org

- Peterson, Roger Tory. *Peterson Field Guide to Birds of North America*. Boston: Houghton Mifflin Harcourt, 2008.

- Peterson, Roger Tory. *Peterson Field Guide to Moths of Northeastern North America*. Boston: Houghton Mifflin Harcourt, 2012.

- Wilson, Joseph S., and Olivia Messinger Carril. *The Bees in Your Backyard: A Guide to North America's Bees*. Princeton, NJ: Princeton University Press, 2015.

Garden and Nature Books

- Bailey, Elisabeth Tova. *The Sound of a Wild Snail Eating*. Chapel Hill, NC: Algonquin Books, 2016.

- Brown, Lauren. *Weeds and Wildflowers in Winter*. New York: W. W. Norton & Company, 2012.

- Capon, Brian. *Botany for Gardeners*. Portland, OR: Timber Press, 2010.

- Chamovitz, Daniel. *What a Plant Knows: A Field Guide to the Senses*. New York: Farrar, Straus and Giroux, 2012.